CW00552605

Bobby Nayyar was born in Handsworth, Birmingham in 1979. He read French and Italian at Trinity College, Cambridge. He has been published in the *Mango Shake* and *Too Asian, Not Asian Enough* anthologies, and journals including *Wasafiri* and *Aesthetica*.

He founded Limehouse Books in 2009, publishing his debut novel, *West of No East* in 2011, and *The No Salaryman* two years later. *Glass Scissors* is his debut poetry collection.

He lives in London.

bobbynayyar.com

GLASS SCISSORS

Also by Bobby Nayyar

West of No East
The No Salaryman

GLASS SCISSORS

BOBBY NAYYAR

LIMEHOUSE
BOOKS

To Uršulia

Moi, dis-je, et c'est assez.

—*Médée*, Corneille

CONTENTS

Into the Blue Forest

PREFACE

After the release of my debut novel *West of No East* in 2011, I stopped writing for a couple of years.

I wanted to think about what sort of writer I wanted to be, which is like deciding what sort of life I wanted to lead. There had been a series of events from my past that I wanted to explore, and memories much deeper that had risen to the surface.

I had always wanted to write a poetry collection, but remain averse to calling myself a poet. It is a loaded word, and I'm not sure I want to carry its weight. After 36 years I am confident that I am a writer; what *type* of writer is always evolving.

As I developed my ideas for *Glass Scissors,* I soon decided to combine elements of theatre and music into the structure of the book. The collection consists of three movements pulsing towards a crescendo, which was one of the trigger points that set me on this journey when I was a teenager. To that end, it would be best if you read the book in sequence from beginning to end.

Glass Scissors is a journey that starts with the heart but ends with the mind, because when all is said and done, the actions resultant from our thoughts are what will endure.

Bobby Nayyar

LOVE

&

THUNDER

Setting the Page

I've sat before this page for 36 years,
Watching it pixelate from paper and ink,
My eyes now reinforced by glass,
My mind broken two times,
My heart three,
And counting.

I stare into its screen
Until all I see are
Blades of ice slicing my past.
My hopes and fears,
Like layers of clothing
Worn on a day turned warm.
I'll sweat knowing that
The half-life of memory
Will decay into the afterlife of words.

And through the pain of my wounds self-inflicted,
The loves lost and found repeatedly,
The dirt of work
And strength of family,
The words rise.

And now I realise
That this page was never blank.
My scissors,
Forever cutting.

Advice to a Schoolboy

You won't find what you're looking for on Google,
Wikipedia or Bing. You can't Snapchat, WhatsApp
or Ask.fm it.
And yes, I notice every time you glance at your BB.
But don't worry.
I'll just grumble and say,
'We didn't have those things in my day'.

You see what they do at school is give you spoons,
And ask you to chew, rinse and spit.
It's not the teachers' fault,
They work much more than you'll ever see,
With less than you'll believe.
It's only when you're my age you realise
That intelligence isn't about what you know,
It's about how you think.

I don't remember my youth,
I'm too far gone for that.
But I still remember what it's like to be young:
The dislike of authority,
The desire for autonomy,
The crushes and tumbles into love each and every day.
But as much as you swagger
And curse under your breath,
I won't bend.
Because I've been you,
And I'm still here.

I know why you want to conquer:
The rage of hormones mixed with
Expectations of the man you're meant to be.

Use it.

Weren't Odysseus and Heracles the
Iron Man and Hulk of their time?
Such is the tendency for men to mythologise,
From what boys have dreamed.

I$

Art is the science of the soul,
But I don't know if I'm a scientist.
There's a minority of things in my control,
Just to prove that I exist.

That I am matter
That matters.
I have a voice
And a choice
To qualify
The look in your eyes
And depth of your sigh
In words that will last
Far longer than you or I.

I am an artist,
Not a philanthropist!

What I do has great value
And I'm not going to sell it for free
Or exchange it for reasonable expenses
No,
Not anymore.

Capitalism needs Art
To show that the accumulation of wealth
Isn't all that bad.
We being the dull edge of that sword.

Now Art needs Capitalism
So we can survive the cuts,
Perfect our craft
Not graft through grant applications.
Painting KPIs and
Pimping ourselves
To all the bad things that make money
And do harm to the planet.

This isn't a poem,
It's an omen!

She is

Without owning a single photograph of her,
You believe she looks like a cross between
Stana Katić and Edita Vilkevičiūtė.
Such is the tendency to associate
The memory of beauty
With the beauty of sight.
'A pretty girl,' she calls herself,
But she is much more than that.

She is the hardness in how she speaks,
Which is harder than life itself.
The pointed syllables that
Upon occasion have needled your pride,
And left tiny scars across the atria of your heart.

She is the way she sees herself inverted
To everything you've ever said she is.
As if all this time you've not been talking to her,
But to her self reflected in a mirror
Forged by your anxiety and doubt.

She is a sadness concealed in a sigh,
Swallowed whole in apology.
The rarity of her smile,
And the embers in her eyes
Falling in footsteps beside you.

As you age you begin to see
That the purpose of growing older

Is not only to love,
It is to be loved.
As distance bounds each passing year,
And what beats in her heart,
And rides in her soul eludes you.
You know you will follow,
If she calls,
Because she is.

The Lesser of Three Evils

1.

I will vote,
Not in protest,
Or resignation,
But in hope.
Hope that there is an end in sight
To rhetoric.
That our lives are more than pebbles
To be thrown
With one eye closed.
As our country creeps closer
To the Land of the Free,
Where politics is not red or blue,
But darkest green.

2.

Like faith,
Politics depends upon the belief that
The greater good will prevail
In spite of all the evidence to the contrary.
That the spirit seemingly limitless
In its corruptibility,
Will correct itself
(After it gets caught).
But faith is the water
That circles the drain.
It is the skein that knots the abyss.

3.

And even though it runs against logic,
As parody becomes politic,
What else is there to do,
But vote?
If all we are is an
'X' etched on a paper
Buried in a box
And
Forgotten
For
Five
More
Years.

Sometimes the Madness is Worth It

Don't text her,
Don't call,
Don't you dare write her a letter.
Compose yourself, not a message.
Breathe.

Look back,
Because back then wasn't so great.
You have a habit of processing memories like
A factory processes meat.
The constant grinding sparking thunder in your
hippocampus,
Chalk on your tongue,
Bitterness tipped against the sweet.

It drips down you know,
To that place in your soul,
Where longing pools.
The days become weeks,
The cerulean contracts,
Until there is no more.
Except words.

So use it.
Write that book,
Script that play,
Finish this poem.

And remember that in the end,
It isn't about her,
Your muse by absence,
It's about you.

Pieces of Glass

She moves her hand and says,
'Throw it in there'.
The intimacy of her handbag lost
In the loneliness of pubs,
Screw-top wine and Premiership football.

To interrupt the silence she takes his glasses.
The horizontal metal frame complementing the angles
Of her cheek and jaw.
'How do I look?'
'You look like a teacher'.
'I can see you clearly now'.
'How did you see me before?'
She pauses. The thin mettle of her lips closing,
As she reaches for balm.

'I wear glass to flatten my eyes'.
'Severe astigmatism,' she explains.
She can see as far as the door, but not
To the street outside where the red of tail lights are met
By the passing blue of ambulances.
'I see just as far as I need to. Nothing more'.
'Like a shield that no man sees,' he comments,
As she refuses a touch.

He can see to the bus stop, where they will wait
For her to go home.
To flowers and red wine,
And walks along the river.

The lamp in his bedroom,
Placed on the floor,
Her head in his hands, caressed by kisses,
The flex of her torso, as she dresses in haste.
The books and the papers strewn on his desk.
Pulled fingerprints through dust
On the top of picture frames.

'Arsenal have just scored,' she says and
Takes off his glasses. The blue in her
Eyes reminding him of the pit of a volcano.

She's Settling Down

1.

There's nothing more painful
Than truth over coffee.
The overpour of words in
The tightest of spaces.
Starbucks was never built for this.

You listen and watch as
The pathways of your life and hers
Diverge with every sip.
The could, the would and the should,
Swallowed whole with the dregs.
Yet the steel in her jaw,
Mixed with the tender vulnerability in which she speaks
Make it impossible to look away.

Her eyes have never looked as blue,
And the smile she wears
Is something new.
The curve of her lips
Carry a double-edged truth:
She is happy,
And this happiness means that
You have to let her go.

2.

The women you have loved,
You will always love.
In the infinite spaces
Of your mind and
The sinews of your heart.
Where promises test
The time that passes,
And autumnal drifts
Beckon the end of summer
A little earlier each year.

3.

She leaves you
With a kiss on your cheek
To wear through every season.

The
THEATRE
of
UNREST

What happens next will not blow your mind

The hesitation you have before you click
Is the wonder of where your life might have been
And where it is going.

What you could achieve while
The time of your life
Is clicking away.

It's not even the big things:
Falling in love;
Authoring that masterpiece;
Creating new life.

It's the little things:
Talking to people;
Lifting your head up to catch the horizon;
Moving your body beyond the inertia of your mind.

No tricks.
No hacks.
No easy solutions to long-lived problems.
Nothing will blow your mind.
Except for a gun,
Or some really good drugs.

London

I don't want to grow old in this city.
This city that builds itself,
On the backs of the poor.

I don't want to see myself as an old man riding the Tube,
Struggling to stand still,
Sighing to be offered a seat.

As I age,
I think more and more of my Father
Bent sweating, trying to tie his shoelaces
Around the bulb of his stomach,
Before he starts his twelve-hour shift.
The accumulation of his sixty one years
Pent up in that mass surrounded by thrift.
Thrift I could never imagine
Or practice.

For I have no pension.
I have no savings.
I have no wealth to breed wealth.
When the time comes
I will fall into the sea,
And my limbs
Can feed
A thousand fishes.

Grammar

Her language has no definite
Or indefinite article
It explains so much.

We talk in clauses,
Not knowing if we are
A, or *the, or none at all.*
Our words weighted by
Gravity, like interpretation.

Plans made in the simple future
Complicated by our past historic.
From week to week
Our grammar repeats
One kiss on the cheek
Or two,
Or none at all?

She says that I live in the past
Tense,
But the past is no place.
It is a broken mirror
Scattered everywhere,
Splinters of glass in my feet,
Hurting more when I walk,
So I run and bleed.

Our understanding only aligns,
When the language we speak
Becomes the language of touch.
In lieu of ellipsis,
Her body tightens
Reality intervenes
Her verb changes.
And we are left to forgive the faults
Of our distractions.
Me for you,
You for me.

Aphorismal

I've been rich and I've been poor,
Being rich was definitely better.

The challenge of modern life
Is to discern between want and need.

Those who are good at building
Are better at destroying.

The best rioting I did
Was around a boardroom table.

A truth told is a partial truth,
A truth written is a partial lie.

Some of the best decisions I've made
Were when I was completely wired out of my skull.

Work for others and the knives are at your back,
Work for yourself and the knives are at your throat.

That's the problem with young people,
They make everyone around them look old.

Even in this digital age,
What is real is
What can be seen by the naked eye,
And the naked eye alone.

The smaller the lens,
The smaller the subject.

Our addictions become the legs
Upon which we stand.

The Journey

Her name is a journey
Starting east
But not as east as you,
She whispers a roar
From Warsaw to Siberia.
Heart embedded in ice
Abject in honesty yet
Solipsistic with truth.
She speaks of her duties,
Which you interpret as love.

You have traced her genealogy
Through books:
Dostoevsky, Chekhov and Bulgakov.
Yet you know her no more
Than you know yourself.
As foreign as the Sun,
And the water-soaked ravines of Mars.
She is an immigrant
Like your parents,
But not like you.
She understands survival,
And sacrifice,
With no net to fall on
And no siblings to call on
Unlike you.

You connect with her
In respect of the journey.
Heeding the call that compels you east
To the outlands of your heart.

Oh the Indignation!

☺

After the electrocution of
7th May 2015
I passed a few days
Recanting in horror
That I had perpetuated
The vicious lie
That my voice mattered.

☺

The months of build up,
Showers of digital hope
Upon metropolitan lines.

This wasn't:

OBAMA HOPE

There was no screen-print to plaster on ghetto walls
Just a man much more awkward,
As I turned from yellow to red.

☺

Democracy depends upon the belief
That every person makes a difference
And has a voice
And believes that things can change.
I was wrong,
So wrong.

All my Facebook friends were wrong
All my Twitter followers were wrong
Google+?
Wrong!

☺

We had conned ourselves into believing
That we could speak with our thumbs
Whilst forgetting our tongues,
And our feet,
And our hands.
The body politic reduced
To a digit, not even a proper finger.

☹

After the numbness had passed
I saw that London was its own island
And that England
Really was this 'happy breed of men'
Who cared about their homes and their money
They were there *en masse*
To make sure that
Those much younger than I
Would have no future.

☹

So where does this leave me?
I could change my profile pic,
Like anyone gives a shit.
I could take to the streets,
But I don't have the feet.

☹

I'll just watch it happen again and again
The posts as they stray
Right now Corbyn, Cecil and Calais
And I will swear
And write
And do nothing.

😐zzz

I Pity the Poor Publisher

My first week on the job
In the splendour of Brettenham House,
I stood on carpeted floors by marble walls
Waiting for the lift.

I didn't know who he was until a few days later,
The dapper man with silver hair
Who approached me cautiously
And stood and stared at my reflection
In the polished lift doors
Like I might ask him for the time
So I could steal his watch.

From floor to floor
We rode on down,
At opposite ends
Of opposite lives.
Brought together by what I had thought
Was a love of books.

Yet after all these years
And so many lost memories
Why do I still remember
This triviality?

Just another entry in my
Catalogue of disgusted looks,
On my journey in and out of
The publishing industry.

This ivory tower made open plan
By greed and stupidity,
And a clan who have clung on to power
At the expense of youth, colour and difference.
Only to find the matter of truth that
The world has moved on,
And they are the ones burning.

The look on your face

The train jagged on the tracks,
Then hiccoughed to a stop.
The unwanted shock
Compounding the misery of a morning commute,
Beneath Piccadilly.

I remember it clearly because it was the first time
You looked at my face.

It was a month after the bombs,
Six years after the planes.
The Western world once more covered in dust,
And soot that once clung to the darkness
Of Victorian walls.

It was the day I tried to walk to work,
Until I saw those who had travelled before me
Staggering against the tide with blood on their faces.

The train came to a stop.
You held your stare
On me.
I could taste your bitterness
And fear.

Yet when the train reopened its doors then
Began to move,
You returned to your paper and
I was forgotten once more.

But still I remember.

It wasn't the way that you looked at me
That worries me still.
It is the way you looked past me,
And looked through me
Out on the street when times were fairer,
And we might have been acquaintances,
Or even friends.

A look as if I have never existed
Or touched upon your life
As you had touched upon mine.

Tether

We emerged from the labyrinth
Beneath Nagoya train station
And rode the escalators
As high as we could go

Emerging to a room walled with glass
We steadied ourselves amidst a throng of
Steel-tipped buildings, which stood
Like a forest spearing the sky

Holding globes of blinking red lights
The trees offered a warning
To planes and Gods alike
I stood and stared,
As you left me to the night.

Those blinking red lights
Have followed me my whole life
Caught by their glare
A line drawn by their sight
To a darkness of the soul
A notification not to be alone
When I should be sleeping,
I check my phone.

Another Man

We walked the Tate Britain twice.
You wanted to see Emin's bed,
I wanted to see you.

Dressed in black like
You were attending a funeral.
Your feet in ballet flats.
You had never looked so small
And imposing.

A cloud about to spark,
You pointed at *The Lady of Shalott*
Then *Ophelia* and said,
'I bet you like those paintings'.
I nodded then pointed to the Rossetti's.
You didn't speak,
Your breath a rumble of thunder.

Trying to prove myself
I took you to *Chatterton*.
We stood and stared
From floor to bed
To dead body and St Paul's.
I read the line from Marlowe
And realised that we were
Two branches
Cut from the same tree.

Our time was up,
You left to go to him.
I walked to Trafalgar Square
And let the crowds push me
In every direction.

I scratched the places I wanted you to see
And the people I hoped for you to meet.

To show you that I am more
Than another man
An also ran
An hour and a half
A pot of tea.

And then I wrote this for you
To discover how much you can create
From someone you love,
As much as you hate.

The black guy gets it

He was the best of them:
Barrel-chested
Philosophic,
A hammer hanging from his belt,
A titan among lesser gods.

Yet there he stood,
Disarmed by a photograph,
Bitten by a boy
Who approached
In a vacuum of violence.

It was not enough that
Tyreese was slain by a boy,
He also had to be tortured
By the demons of his past,
As he lay dying.

It reminded me that
The black guy gets it
Sooner or later.
And again, and again
Never to be one
Of the central cast
Not a Daryl,
Or even a Glenn.

I am not a black man
Yet I am a black man
This you must understand.
The racism I bear
Reminds me of who I am:
An Englishman.

A year in the Land of the Free
Living off 53rd street
I heard gunshots
Echoing through the night.
A decade on
The only way I can
Process these events
Is through fiction
Because the facts are too hard to bear:
How can you fight
A bullet in the back?
As the bodies caught
Through the smallest of lenses
Begin to stack and
Force the gentle to see
That the violence was always here
Hidden in that vacuum
Waiting to strike.

The Crash (2008)

I never saw it coming.
Like the employees of Lehman Brothers,
Who in the end carried their lives out
In cardboard boxes,
Coffins to their careers.
Mourning in silence.

Eating cereal riding the Tube
No thought no music
Words like gravel
Beneath my fingertips
Typing emails with no meaning
So much grieving
For so little grief.

And then repeat.

Panic in my throat
Fear in my feet
A mind formerly still
Forced into motion
Toecaps past the yellow line
Peering onto the tracks

I had become a subprime
Having borrowed too much self-capital
That I couldn't pay back
And in retrospect
What I remember most

Is that I had zero desire
I wanted for nothing
I lived for no one
Liberated from the pursuit of wealth
The silver lining for this loss of health.

What did I do?

I asked for help.

INTO
THE
BLUE
FOREST

thunderstorms

It was sleep
Sleep
The last refuge
To crystallise what was happening to me.
In a dream
My mind electric
My body pulsing
Floating above purple clouds
And below the dying light of every constellation
Undulating and proud
I saw sky folded in on sky
Clouds mirrored
And firing at each other
With lightning
There was no thunder
Only strobes of light
Then an immense sound
That shook every bone
Every neurone.
I felt my brain crack
An actual crack
Like the grey matter scarred
Was now cleft
A seizure inside strobing light
Everything about me bisected.

Before this happened
I never knew my mind existed
It was weightless

Silent
Living in an abyss
Of happy memories and
Occasional nightmares
Love and hope
Cleanliness and soap.

Now it was a weight I carried
Everywhere I was
Stones in my sockets
Pebbles in my pockets
My feet in every sea.

Two thousand days have passed
And still bearing intense pain
I am every thunderstorm
That has passed
My mind tectonic.

The Questions

Short-sleeved shirt in winter?
The doctor looks as sick as me,
Scratching at his forearm,
As I start to tell him how I feel.

He turns to his computer
– They always turn to their computer –
And I start to wonder why
I didn't just stay at home and use Google.

Tapping with stubby index fingers
He then waits for a webpage to load,
Silence filling the technical pauses of the NHS
Before he turns the scroll wheel of his mouse:

Have you found little pleasure or interest in doing things?

Yes.

Have you found yourself feeling down, depressed or hopeless?

Yes.

Have you had trouble falling or staying asleep, or sleeping too much?

Yes.

Each moment is a communion between me,
The doctor and his computer.
Turning back and forth
We pray together.

Have you been feeling tired or had little energy?

Yes.

Have you had a poor appetite or been overeating?

Yes.

*Have you felt that you're a failure or let yourself or your
family down?*

Yes.

It feels like he's telling me
A story of myself.
I am a reader
And I am written.

*Have you had some trouble concentrating on things like
reading the paper or watching TV?*

Yes.

*Have you been moving or speaking slowly, or been very
fidgety, so that other people could notice?*

Yes.

I can't keep still to this interrogation.
I know it is leading to something
Signposted in the furrows of his brow
And pink scratches on his arm
The final question,
The hinge to this trapdoor:

Have you thought that you'd be better off dead or
hurting yourself in some way?

Well.
What does it mean to say 'Yes'?
Does it mean I won't be able to go home?
Will I be taken to some place else?
I lie.
I life.
I want it back.

He knows.
I know.
But still he clicks.
Then by rote
He tells me what I have to do
Next.

Cut

She was Irish
She had to be Irish
This nurse
Who sat in the adjoining office
To the psychiatrist.

Before the medicine
After the thunderstorms
I sat in the dock
Submerged by the pressures of time
The gaze of green eyes
Heavy-set and sullen
Stern and silent,
She expected me to speak
And tell her what was wrong.

'I feel like my brain has split in two. Here'.
I pressed fingers against my forehead.
'Like my brain is cracked'.
Hard like a broken stone
That is growing inside my skull
Pushing force in all directions
Inside me.

No movement in her face
She wrote something on a piece of paper
A show of control

If nothing else
Then in that drawl
As cutting as it was philosophic:
'In all my years I've never heard someone say that'.

In the deluge of the vulnerable,
We must plead for sickness,
As much as our health
I affirmed my condition,
The pain and weight in my skull increasing.

Threshold passed
Her eyes lightened
The harshness of her voice
Those guttural syllables
Softened as she looked
Upon me with compassion.

'This isn't the first time I've heard this,'
She said, as a reward to her test.
'There was a woman, some years back...'
The rest of the memory faded
As I tuned out her voice
She believed me
And that was all that mattered.

Is much of mental health
The divination of truth
Of the human condition?

What is hidden
In plain sight of the endless terrain of
Our minds
The black rocks covered in moss
Volcanic ash and flowers that bloom
In winter as much as spring.

Prescriptions

Between friendship and love
There are conversations that
Thread truth like water
Gripped by hands and hearts
Until there is nothing left to hold.

She asked me if I had ever done anything bad
Clearly wanting to know the spectrum of my humanity
To compare to her spectrum of depravity
Deviant sex?
A crime?
Drugs?
I said, 'No' and drank some more coffee
We were in a Harvester with bad service.

Disappointed she spoke at length
About cannabis and cocaine
A mischievous glint in her eye
I took to mean that she had lived
While I had been dead for so long
I tried to fake a yawn
To show how much she bored me.

Deciding that only an excess of truth
Would kill the conversation
I looked her deep in the eyes and said:
'You want to know why I don't take
Drugs that mess with my brain?'
She nodded.

She knew about the depressions
But was undecided if it was a real condition
Or just a first world way of excusing failure.
'Even when I was young
I never felt the inclination to take drugs,' I said,
'And then when I first got sick my doctor prescribed me
A medicine,
A pill,
To increase the level of serotonin in my brain.
I've been taking it ever since,
I've tried to stop,
But something bad has always happened
When I was going through the withdrawal.'

The lines of her face fell
As if I had just confessed to a bout of
Drug-fuelled murderous gay sex
Sullen,
Her lips pursing
Eyes clouding over,
She growled, 'Oh Bobby,
You have to stop taking those drugs'.

I swallowed more weak tepid coffee
Hoping it would cleanse the thrash of irony from my throat
This doped and coked woman I had loved upon occasion
Was now looking at me as if I was an addict
And she was a saint.

The Crash (2013)

The first time it happened,
I put it down to bad luck.
Nothing more than
A puberty of the mind.
A watershed of dry tears
To know that the energy
That flows through my mind

Could tear me apart,
Deconstruct my identity,
And hide my memories.

I had been humbled.

But as the years passed
In the slipstream of recovery,
I forgot how I happened.

Money,
The shortcut to respect
Was in short supply.
Thick polluted air
I forced myself to breathe.
Unlike Libor
I couldn't be fixed.

The second time
Was all about speed:
Speed of thought,

Speed of emotion,
The mind electric.
The body kinetic.
My soul on fire.

The pendulum that swings
Inside me broke free.
It's all there
The memories.
Words so verbose
Gestures exaggerated
I would have believed in anything
In God
In Love
In Trust.

Not knowing
If the sirens
Were outside
Or in my mind
I roared as I crashed.
Laughing as I fell
At the price we pay
For cash.

Crucible

The measure of this pain
This colouring of the mind
With chemical imbalance
Enables me to touch the tip
Of greatness as I fall.

Afraid of the light
As much the dark
Laying down words
Like children to sleep
Scorning good looks and belonging
Knowing what I am capable of.

Traffic lights that only change
When no cars are coming
A prophet for profit
Writing such beauty
Whilst feeling so ugly
Sympathy never confused with respect.

Writing an accumulation of life
To affirm the fear
That I am dying inside
Glassy-eyed and sighing
Siphoning fire from the sun
In this vessel
I will stay.

Glass Scissors

In indeterminable middle age
Childhood becomes a collection of days.
Emotional spikes that test
A child's capacity to forget.

An ocean
Of love and loved,
My imagination crawls
Through memories unforgotten:

Morning in silence
Eating cereal before school
The sugar rush beneath
The creaking ceiling
Of parents sleeping.

There is a window
Wide and expressive
Overlooking a garden
Of grass and weeds
Dandelions and moss.

In the dim in-between
I was seated,
When the window hammered
Shook assaulted
By a crow flown majestic
Into the pane.

Recoiling onto the patio
The bird lay in a daze
Before rising to caw
And fly away.
Its broad imprint
On the window,
Greasy yet detailed,
Its wings full extent,
Head turned to the right,
Beak pointing towards the sun.

Such an oversight
For a beast
To fly so low
Believing
It was on the right path.

The mark remained
On the window for weeks.
Mother reasoning that
This newly stained glass
Would keep our living room
From further catastrophe.

..
The love of a parent runs deep
While the love between parents
Remains a mystery.
Biology creating life
Life creating love
Love creating new life.

But at night,
When all is quiet
The sound remains
Of something clawing
Behind closed doors.
How the mothers must suffer,
And the fathers endure.

...

The utility room
Lost its perfume of machine oil,
Synthetic wax and the white
Cotton-like filler of cheap jackets.
Mother's industrial sewing machine
Redundant beneath cobwebs
Her scissors filling the space
Where her hands should have been,
Heavy and oversized like two daggers
It lay with blades parted at the tip,
Lips waiting to be kissed.

Father worked the dayshift
And then the nightshift
Mornings a sprint
To make him tea
Before he fell asleep.
Head tipping but never
Falling to the floor.

Without knowing the words
You believe that love is absolute.
Trapped in suburbia

Where trees over lean roads
And houses surround themselves
With moats of concrete.
You walk to school
Watching the school run
Grind traffic to a halt.

....

Another morning
Another outpouring of cereal
This time marked
By the rising tide of milk
Bringing a sleeping moth
To the surface.

It must have been in the box
For a night or two
Now crawling on my cornflakes
Another misguided beast
Believing it had found refuge.

Wings laden in white
It struggled to escape.
I watched it die
Then went to school.
The death of an animal
Not much more than
Two flakes of skin
Follows me still.

.....
The history of our lives
Is the hurt you feel
In the loneliness
Of bathroom breaks.

Believing in faith
But not religions
Knowing that men made gods
And gods made men.

To be a father,
I must be a son.
My mother's son.

......
They came to stay
For an indefinite period of time
Their smell of otherness,
Clinging to the wallpaper.
Baked dust and spices,
Old clothes dried in the sun.
Pungent and allusive
Of the world your parents came from.

They came to start a new life
A man and wife seeking refuge
In your home.
But you had no idea
What it would do
To the fabric of your life.

Mother accepted it withdrawn,
Like money from a bank.
The previous weeks' warning
That something was wrong
Lost in the ocean's song.

....
Mother Father
Wife Husband
A younger mirror
Now you see
Why the pieces fell
Where they fell
It wasn't illness,
It was family.

Months passed
You only remember the days
The slow moving hand
Of history
Erased by the other.

....
They came to stay
For an indefinite period of time
Their smell of otherness,
Washed and laundered,
The sofa where they slept at night
And blankets dry cleaned.
I lost sight of her then,
Gone from the living room
The utility and the garden.

It is impossible to divide
The invisible.
In the kitchen
The sickness accrued.

....

Memoir crystalline,
Kitchen fan laden with grease
Whirring in duress,
As the other wife made roti
For the two families.

Dinner passing in silence
Bitter roti buttered,
Dhal thick and coarse.
The unmarked mirror cracking
With each bite.

Mother went to bed too early
To sleep.

....

There is no sensor to pinpoint
How many days passed.
No app to flashback.

At some point the visitors left.

....

School morning
In the world upstairs
Barefoot carpeted tread
I stepped into the bathroom.

My mother stood
At the mirror
Her long black scissors
In hand
As she held a lock,
Which she cut.
It fell to the sink.

My presence registered
She turned
And smiled
And continued cutting
Her hair.

There was a sea in her eyes
With its own heaven and hell.

I recoiled,
And someone stepped in
To stop
Her.

....
What if Samson was a woman?

....
In the twin blades
I saw myself reflected.
Not as I was then
But as I am now
And will always be.

Burning behind my eyes,
Thunder in mind,
Silence of a mind gone still.

....

Mother changed
Back and forth
Her being in flux
Day by month
Month by year.

The scissors were placed
In a drawer and buried
Beneath papers and
Carrier bags.
And we never spoke
Of what had happened.

Never conceptualised
Or analysed
Or felt we needed
To come to terms
Or ask for words
We could look up
In a dictionary
Just to be sure
Of what we were.

She was better
We were better
And in the pulsations
Of youth we forgot

Only to remember,
When it happened to us.

....
It has taken me all these years
To understand
That I'm not sick,
There is nothing broken
Nothing to fix,
No contagion
No tumour.
Just the understanding of
My self.

To love
To be kind
Not to hurt knowingly.
To be thoughtful
To let hate burn out brightly
Before lasting damage is done.

And remember
That the brilliance
Of these sparks,
These glass scissors,
Is who I am.

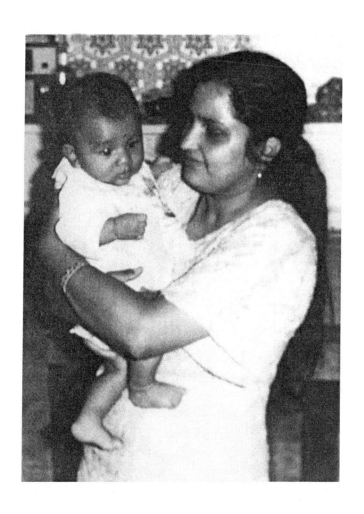

AUTHOR'S NOTE

Today is Friday 27 November 2015 – an empty vote to come on bombing Syria, Adele conquering the planet through heartbreak and the mass exploitation of the poor with Black Friday. In a way these three events reflect the stories I've told in this book.

There is the disease of consumerism, which was the first thing to go when I suffered my initial bout of depression. I had no desire and without desire there is no love, no hate, and no wanting. There is only the bare needs of survival.

Since the financial crash of 2008 the theatre of politics has become increasingly evident. Parliament used to be a West End production, which has been upgraded to opera: loud and colourful but a spectacle where you have no idea what's actually being said. Theatre – this appearance of reality now extends to the financial sector with a crash that has only helped to widen the gap between the rich and the poor. In my first novel I tried to understand if protest could effect change. Four years later and in good health, I see the emptiness in political might that I saw in myself when I was convalescing. But that doesn't mean that we should give up hope.

The third story of *Glass Scissors* is love. The destructive powers of love and also its creative powers. Ultimately this scientist of the soul is just a person who wants to love and be loved. The love poems in this book are like scattered ashes drifting between these two points. I hope that as a whole *Glass Scissors* is a book that captures the experience of loving, falling and living through hard times.

*

After I finished *West of No East* the day before it needed to go to print, I told myself that I would never do that again. Oops I did it again. This is not by design just the calamity of trying to do too many things whilst treading water to pay bills. Aside from the final poem, this book has been proofread. I apologise if there are any typos. It has been a difficult to write about my experiences of depression. The foundation of writing is life experience and now I have detailed the most important events of the last seven years. The situation is complicated by the final poem, as I have written about events from my family history. They say it's easier to seek forgiveness than permission – I have forged ahead hoping that this doesn't burn me or anyone else. The beauty is in the truth to paraphrase Keats.

I don't normally acknowledge anyone, I'm mean that way. But in this exceptional situation there are some exceptional people to give thanks. Firstly my family for supporting me over the last few years as I have drifted from ship to shore. In particular I have to thank my mother for being OK with me writing this book and including her, and also for her and my brother agreeing to use an image of them on the cover (yep, that baby is not me). I'd also like to thank Neil for being there for both crashes and giving helpful feedback on several of these poems. I'd like to thank Katrina for putting up with the production of this book and other titles no doubt. Finally, I would like to thank Ula for starting me on this journey, which has now come to an end.

LIMEHOUSE BOOKS TITLES

2010

100
Bloody Vampires
33 East
33 West
Boys & Girls

2011

West of No East
Men & Women
Exit Through The Wound

2012

After My Own Heart
The Rules of Poker

2013

Briony Hatch

2014

The Pearliad
Highlights of My Last Regret
Thinkless
Freelancer's Diary 2015

2015

(Nothing due to late running of *Glass Scissors*)

2016

Glass Scissors
The Open Pen Anthology
Love Notes to Men Who Don't Read

PATRONS

I am grateful to the following people who pre-ordered *Glass Scissors* directly from Limehouse Books:

Aurelia Seidlhofer
Delia Babiciu
Elisa Bazzani
Eliza Kaczynska-Nay
Emily Foster
Imran Sadiq
Laila Cohen
Raj Lal
Rathin Choudhury
Rukhsana Yasmin
Sameera Hamid
Sanjay Nayyar
Sharon Nayyar
Sinead Turner
Sunita Sharma

A LIMEHOUSE BOOKS PUBLICATION

Written by Bobby Nayyar
Design by Katrina Clark
Additional design by Emily Foster

Typeset in Adobe Caslon Pro and OSP DIN

First published 28.01.2016

ISBN 978-1-9075-3679-3

Limehouse Books
Flat 30, 58 Glasshouse Fields
London E1W 3AB

limehousebooks.co.uk

Printed by Short Run Press Limited

Distributed in North America by SCB Distributors and in the UK and EU by Turnaround.